"MY HEART HAS HEARD YOU SAY,
'COME AND TALK WITH ME.'
AND MY HEART RESPONDS,
'LORD, I AM COMING.'"

Psalm 27:8

HOW TO USE THIS BOOK

Set aside time each day to discover...study... enjoy... learn... God's Word. By following the Bible reading plan in the front of this book, you will read through Galatians, Ephesians, Philippians, Colossians, 1 &2 Thessalonians, 1&2 Timothy, Titus, and Philemon!

You can copy a verse you want to think on, look up definitions to words you are curious about, draw a picture, write a prayer, record what you learned, write down questions you have, etc.

You have a Heavenly Father who loves you and wants to speak to you! Take time to listen to and enjoy relationship with Him.

Write down a verse that really stuck out to you

Look at the Bible reading list to see what passage you are reading next

Look up the definitions to words

Today's Bible Reading: EPHESIANS 6:10-18

"PUT ON ALL OF GOD'S ARMOR SO THAT YOU WILL BE ABLE TO STAND FIRM AGAINST ALL THE STRATEGIES OF THE DEVIL." VERSE 11

STRATEGIES: A CAREFUL PLAN OR METHOD; THE ART OF PLANNING MILITARY OPERATIONS IN A WAR OR BATTLE

NOTES

HOW DO I PUT ON GOD'S ARMOR?

SALVATION
GOD'S WORD
GOD'S RIGHTEOUSNESS
TRUTH
FAITH
PEACE

Write down your questions

Take notes, summarize the passage, look up definitions, draw a picture to illustrate a verse, etc.

Draw a picture

QUICK TIPS You don't have to do all these things! But take some time to try to understand what you read and let the Holy Spirit speak to you.

HOW TO USE THIS BOOK

It is very important to develop good habits. Our habits (good and bad) affect who we become.

Some habits are fun, some are boring, some we just have to do because it's part of being a family or taking care of what we have been given.

Write down what you need/want to do each day. Check off the task if you do it.

QUICK TIPS Use stickers or draw pictures to make your planner more fun.

MY DAILY HABITS

- ✗ BRUSH TEETH (A/M/P/M)
- ✗ CLEAN ROOM
- ✗ READ BIBLE
- ✗ PLAY OUTSIDE
- ✗ PRACTICE PIANO FOR 15 MINUTES
- ○ SHOOT 25 LAY-UPS AND FREE THROWS
- ○ TAKE MY DOG ON A WALK
- ○ _____

you can do it

Whether you do this the night before, or soon after waking up, take some time to think through your day. List the time commitments you have, goals/to-do's you want to accomplish, bucket list items, etc.

QUICK TIPS

Talk with your family to find out what is on the schedule, what you need to get done, and make suggestions for fun activities.

THIS MORNING I WILL:

READ MY BIBLE   PRACTICE BASKETBALL

GET MY CHORES DONE !!

THIS AFTERNOON I WILL:

 GO TO THE BEACH!

6:30   GRANDMA COMING FOR DINNER

SUMMER BUCKET LIST

 **QUICK TIPS** Look in the back of this book for a list of things to do if you are bored.

90 DAYS OF SUMMER BIBLE READING

- [ ] Galatians 1:1-10
- [ ] Galatians 1:11-24
- [ ] Galatians 2:1-10
- [ ] Galatians 2:11-21
- [ ] Galatians 3:1-14
- [ ] Galatians 3:15-22
- [ ] Galatians 3:23-29
- [ ] Galatians 4:1-7
- [ ] Galatians 4:8-20
- [ ] Galatians 4:21-31
- [ ] Galatians 5:1-15
- [ ] Galatians 5:16-26
- [ ] Galatians 6:1-10
- [ ] Galatians 6:11-18
- [ ] Ephesians 1:1-14
- [ ] Ephesians 1:15-23
- [ ] Ephesians 2:1-10
- [ ] Ephesians 2:11-22
- [ ] Ephesians 3:1-13
- [ ] Ephesians 3:14-21
- [ ] Ephesians 4:1-5
- [ ] Ephesians 4:6-16
- [ ] Ephesians 4:17-32
- [ ] Ephesians 5:1-14
- [ ] Ephesians 5:15-20
- [ ] Ephesians 5:21-33
- [ ] Ephesians 6:1-4
- [ ] Ephesians 6:5-9
- [ ] Ephesians 6:10-18
- [ ] Ephesians 6:19-24
- [ ] Philippians 1:1-11
- [ ] Philippians 1:12-26
- [ ] Philippians 1:27-30
- [ ] Philippians 2:1-11
- [ ] Philippians 2:12-18
- [ ] Philippians 2:19-30
- [ ] Philippians 3:1-11
- [ ] Philippians 3:12-21
- [ ] Philippians 4:1-9
- [ ] Philippians 4:10-23
- [ ] Colossians 1:1-8
- [ ] Colossians 1:9-14
- [ ] Colossians 1:15-23
- [ ] Colossians 1:24-29
- [ ] Colossians 2:1-5
- [ ] Colossians 2:6-10
- [ ] Colossians 2:11-23
- [ ] Colossians 3:1-11
- [ ] Colossians 3:12-17
- [ ] Colossians 3:18-25
- [ ] Colossians 4:1-6
- [ ] Colossians 4:7-18
- [ ] 1 Thess. 1:1-10
- [ ] 1 Thess. 2:1-13
- [ ] 1 Thess. 2:14-20
- [ ] 1 Thess. 3:1-13
- [ ] 1 Thess. 4:1-12
- [ ] 1 Thess. 4:13-18
- [ ] 1 Thess. 5:1-11
- [ ] 1 Thess. 5:12-28
- [ ] 2 Thess. 1:1-12
- [ ] 2 Thess. 2:1-12
- [ ] 2 Thess. 2:13-17
- [ ] 2 Thess. 3:1-5
- [ ] 2 Thess. 3:6-18
- [ ] 1 Timothy 1:1-11
- [ ] 1 Timothy 1:12-20
- [ ] 1 Timothy 2:1-7
- [ ] 1 Timothy 2:8-15
- [ ] 1 Timothy 3:1-13
- [ ] 1 Timothy 3:14-16
- [ ] 1 Timothy 4:1-16
- [ ] 1 Timothy 5:1-16
- [ ] 1 Timothy 5:17-25
- [ ] 1 Timothy 6:1-10
- [ ] 1 Timothy 6:11-21
- [ ] 2 Timothy 1:1-7
- [ ] 2 Timothy 1:8-18
- [ ] 2 Timothy 2:1-14
- [ ] 2 Timothy 2:15-26
- [ ] 2 Timothy 3:1-9
- [ ] 2 Timothy 3:10-17
- [ ] 2 Timothy 4:1-8
- [ ] 2 Timothy 4:9-22
- [ ] Titus 1:1-9
- [ ] Titus 1:10-16
- [ ] Titus 2:1-5
- [ ] Titus 2:6-15
- [ ] Titus 3:1-15
- [ ] Philemon 1:1-25

DATE _____

S M T W T F S

LORD, THANK YOU...

_____
_____
_____

TODAY'S BIBLE READING:

MY DAILY HABITS

- BRUSH TEETH (AM/PM)
- CLEAN ROOM
- READ BIBLE
- PLAY OUTSIDE
- _____
- _____
- _____
- _____

THIS MORNING I WILL:

THIS AFTERNOON I WILL:

DATE _____

S M T W T F S

LORD, THANK YOU...
_____
_____
_____

TODAY'S BIBLE READING:

MY DAILY HABITS

- BRUSH TEETH (AM/PM)
- CLEAN ROOM
- READ BIBLE
- PLAY OUTSIDE
- _____
- _____
- _____
- _____

THIS MORNING I WILL:

THIS AFTERNOON I WILL:

DATE _____

S M T W T F S

LORD, THANK YOU...
_____
_____
_____

TODAY'S BIBLE READING:

MY DAILY HABITS

- BRUSH TEETH (AM/PM)
- CLEAN ROOM
- READ BIBLE
- PLAY OUTSIDE
- _____
- _____
- _____
- _____

THIS MORNING I WILL:

THIS AFTERNOON I WILL:

DATE _____

S M T W T F S

LORD, THANK YOU...
_____
_____
_____

TODAY'S BIBLE READING:

MY DAILY HABITS

- ○ BRUSH TEETH (AM/PM)
- ○ CLEAN ROOM
- ○ READ BIBLE
- ○ PLAY OUTSIDE
- ○ _____
- ○ _____
- ○ _____
- ○ _____

THIS MORNING I WILL:

THIS AFTERNOON I WILL:

DATE _____

S M T W T F S

LORD, THANK YOU...
_____
_____
_____

TODAY'S BIBLE READING:

MY DAILY HABITS

- BRUSH TEETH (AM/PM)
- CLEAN ROOM
- READ BIBLE
- PLAY OUTSIDE
- _____
- _____
- _____
- _____

THIS MORNING I WILL:

THIS AFTERNOON I WILL:

DATE _____

S M T W T F S

LORD, THANK YOU...
_____
_____
_____

Today's Bible Reading:

My Daily Habits

- BRUSH TEETH (AM/PM)
- CLEAN ROOM
- READ BIBLE
- PLAY OUTSIDE
- _____
- _____
- _____
- _____

This Morning I Will:

This Afternoon I Will:

DATE _____

S M T W T F S

LORD, THANK YOU...
_____
_____
_____

TODAY'S BIBLE READING:

MY DAILY HABITS

- BRUSH TEETH (AM/PM)
- CLEAN ROOM
- READ BIBLE
- PLAY OUTSIDE
- _____
- _____
- _____
- _____

THIS MORNING I WILL:

THIS AFTERNOON I WILL:

Date _____

S M T W T F S

Lord, thank you...
_____
_____
_____

Today's Bible Reading:

My Daily Habits

- ○ Brush Teeth (AM/PM)
- ○ Clean Room
- ○ Read Bible
- ○ Play Outside
- ○ _____
- ○ _____
- ○ _____
- ○ _____

This Morning I Will:

This Afternoon I Will:

DATE _____

S M T W T F S

LORD, THANK YOU...
_____
_____
_____

TODAY'S BIBLE READING:

MY DAILY HABITS

- BRUSH TEETH (AM/PM)
- CLEAN ROOM
- READ BIBLE
- PLAY OUTSIDE
- _____
- _____
- _____
- _____

THIS MORNING I WILL:

THIS AFTERNOON I WILL:

DATE _____

S M T W T F S

LORD, THANK YOU...
_____
_____
_____

TODAY'S BIBLE READING:

MY DAILY HABITS

- BRUSH TEETH (AM/PM)
- CLEAN ROOM
- READ BIBLE
- PLAY OUTSIDE
- _____
- _____
- _____
- _____

THIS MORNING I WILL:

THIS AFTERNOON I WILL:

DATE _____

S M T W T F S

LORD, THANK YOU...
_____
_____
_____

TODAY'S BIBLE READING:

MY DAILY HABITS

- ○ BRUSH TEETH (AM/PM)
- ○ CLEAN ROOM
- ○ READ BIBLE
- ○ PLAY OUTSIDE
- ○ _____
- ○ _____
- ○ _____
- ○ _____

THIS MORNING I WILL:

THIS AFTERNOON I WILL:

DATE _____

S M T W T F S

LORD, THANK YOU...
_____
_____
_____

TODAY'S BIBLE READING:

MY DAILY HABITS

- BRUSH TEETH (AM/PM)
- CLEAN ROOM
- READ BIBLE
- PLAY OUTSIDE
- _____
- _____
- _____
- _____

THIS MORNING I WILL:

THIS AFTERNOON I WILL:

DATE _____

S M T W T F S

LORD, THANK YOU...
_____
_____
_____

TODAY'S BIBLE READING:

MY DAILY HABITS

- BRUSH TEETH (AM/PM)
- CLEAN ROOM
- READ BIBLE
- PLAY OUTSIDE
- _____
- _____
- _____
- _____

THIS MORNING I WILL:

THIS AFTERNOON I WILL:

DATE _____

S M T W T F S

LORD, THANK YOU...

_____
_____
_____

Today's Bible Reading:

My Daily Habits

- ○ BRUSH TEETH (AM/PM)
- ○ CLEAN ROOM
- ○ READ BIBLE
- ○ PLAY OUTSIDE
- ○ _____
- ○ _____
- ○ _____
- ○ _____

This Morning I Will:

This Afternoon I Will:

Date _____

S M T W T F S

LORD, THANK YOU...
_____
_____
_____

Today's Bible Reading:

My Daily Habits

- ○ BRUSH TEETH (AM/PM)
- ○ CLEAN ROOM
- ○ READ BIBLE
- ○ PLAY OUTSIDE
- ○ _____
- ○ _____
- ○ _____
- ○ _____

This Morning I Will:

This Afternoon I Will:

DATE _____

S M T W T F S

LORD, THANK YOU...
_____
_____
_____

TODAY'S BIBLE READING:

MY DAILY HABITS

- ○ BRUSH TEETH (AM/PM)
- ○ CLEAN ROOM
- ○ READ BIBLE
- ○ PLAY OUTSIDE
- ○ _____
- ○ _____
- ○ _____
- ○ _____

THIS MORNING I WILL:

THIS AFTERNOON I WILL:

DATE _____

S M T W T F S

LORD, THANK YOU...
_____
_____
_____

TODAY'S BIBLE READING:

MY DAILY HABITS

- BRUSH TEETH (AM/PM)
- CLEAN ROOM
- READ BIBLE
- PLAY OUTSIDE
- _____
- _____
- _____
- _____

THIS MORNING I WILL:

THIS AFTERNOON I WILL:

DATE _____

S M T W T F S

LORD, THANK YOU...
_____
_____
_____

TODAY'S BIBLE READING:

MY DAILY HABITS

- BRUSH TEETH (AM/PM)
- CLEAN ROOM
- READ BIBLE
- PLAY OUTSIDE
- _____
- _____
- _____
- _____

THIS MORNING I WILL:

THIS AFTERNOON I WILL:

Date _____

S M T W T F S

LORD, THANK YOU...
_____
_____
_____

Today's Bible Reading:

My Daily Habits

- BRUSH TEETH (AM/PM)
- CLEAN ROOM
- READ BIBLE
- PLAY OUTSIDE
- _____
- _____
- _____

This Morning I Will:

This Afternoon I Will:

DATE _____

S M T W T F S

LORD, THANK YOU...
_____
_____
_____

TODAY'S BIBLE READING:

MY DAILY HABITS

- BRUSH TEETH (AM/PM)
- CLEAN ROOM
- READ BIBLE
- PLAY OUTSIDE
- _____
- _____
- _____
- _____

THIS MORNING I WILL:

THIS AFTERNOON I WILL:

DATE _____

S M T W T F S

LORD, THANK YOU...

_____
_____
_____

Today's Bible Reading:

My Daily Habits

- ○ BRUSH TEETH (AM/PM)
- ○ CLEAN ROOM
- ○ READ BIBLE
- ○ PLAY OUTSIDE
- ○ _____
- ○ _____
- ○ _____
- ○ _____

This Morning I Will:

This Afternoon I Will:

DATE _____

S M T W T F S

LORD, THANK YOU...
_____
_____
_____

TODAY'S BIBLE READING:

MY DAILY HABITS

- BRUSH TEETH (AM/PM)
- CLEAN ROOM
- READ BIBLE
- PLAY OUTSIDE
- _____
- _____
- _____
- _____

THIS MORNING I WILL:

THIS AFTERNOON I WILL:

DATE _____

S M T W T F S

LORD, THANK YOU...
_____
_____
_____

TODAY'S BIBLE READING:

MY DAILY HABITS

- ○ BRUSH TEETH (AM/PM)
- ○ CLEAN ROOM
- ○ READ BIBLE
- ○ PLAY OUTSIDE
- ○ _____
- ○ _____
- ○ _____
- ○ _____

THIS MORNING I WILL:

THIS AFTERNOON I WILL:

Date _____

S M T W T F S

LORD, THANK YOU...
_____
_____
_____

Today's Bible Reading:

My Daily Habits

- ○ BRUSH TEETH (AM/PM)
- ○ CLEAN ROOM
- ○ READ BIBLE
- ○ PLAY OUTSIDE
- ○ _____
- ○ _____
- ○ _____
- ○ _____

This Morning I Will:

This Afternoon I Will:

DATE _____

S M T W T F S

LORD, THANK YOU...
_____
_____
_____

TODAY'S BIBLE READING:

MY DAILY HABITS

- BRUSH TEETH (AM/PM)
- CLEAN ROOM
- READ BIBLE
- PLAY OUTSIDE
- _____
- _____
- _____
- _____

THIS MORNING I WILL:

THIS AFTERNOON I WILL:

DATE _____

S M T W T F S

LORD, THANK YOU...
_____
_____
_____

TODAY'S BIBLE READING:

MY DAILY HABITS

- BRUSH TEETH (AM/PM)
- CLEAN ROOM
- READ BIBLE
- PLAY OUTSIDE
- _____
- _____
- _____
- _____

THIS MORNING I WILL:

THIS AFTERNOON I WILL:

DATE _____

S M T W T F S

LORD, THANK YOU...
_____
_____
_____

TODAY'S BIBLE READING:

MY DAILY HABITS

- BRUSH TEETH (AM/PM)
- CLEAN ROOM
- READ BIBLE
- PLAY OUTSIDE
- _____
- _____
- _____

THIS MORNING I WILL:

THIS AFTERNOON I WILL:

DATE _____

S M T W T F S

LORD, THANK YOU...
_____
_____
_____

TODAY'S BIBLE READING:

MY DAILY HABITS

- BRUSH TEETH (AM/PM)
- CLEAN ROOM
- READ BIBLE
- PLAY OUTSIDE
- _____
- _____
- _____
- _____

THIS MORNING I WILL:

THIS AFTERNOON I WILL:

DATE _____

S M T W T F S

LORD, THANK YOU...
_____
_____
_____

TODAY'S BIBLE READING:

MY DAILY HABITS

- ○ BRUSH TEETH (AM/PM)
- ○ CLEAN ROOM
- ○ READ BIBLE
- ○ PLAY OUTSIDE
- ○ _____
- ○ _____
- ○ _____
- ○ _____

THIS MORNING I WILL:

THIS AFTERNOON I WILL:

DATE _____

S M T W T F S

LORD, THANK YOU...
_____
_____
_____

Today's Bible Reading:

MY DAILY HABITS

- BRUSH TEETH (AM/PM)
- CLEAN ROOM
- READ BIBLE
- PLAY OUTSIDE
- _____
- _____
- _____
- _____

THIS MORNING I WILL:

THIS AFTERNOON I WILL:

DATE _____

S M T W T F S

LORD, THANK YOU...
_____
_____
_____

Today's Bible Reading:

My Daily Habits

- BRUSH TEETH (AM/PM)
- CLEAN ROOM
- READ BIBLE
- PLAY OUTSIDE
- _____
- _____
- _____
- _____

This Morning I Will:

This Afternoon I Will:

DATE _____

S M T W T F S

LORD, THANK YOU...
_____
_____
_____

TODAY'S BIBLE READING:

MY DAILY HABITS

- BRUSH TEETH (AM/PM)
- CLEAN ROOM
- READ BIBLE
- PLAY OUTSIDE
- _____
- _____
- _____
- _____

THIS MORNING I WILL:

THIS AFTERNOON I WILL:

DATE _____

S M T W T F S

LORD, THANK YOU...
_____
_____
_____

TODAY'S BIBLE READING:

MY DAILY HABITS

- ○ BRUSH TEETH (AM/PM)
- ○ CLEAN ROOM
- ○ READ BIBLE
- ○ PLAY OUTSIDE
- ○ _____
- ○ _____
- ○ _____
- ○ _____

THIS MORNING I WILL:

THIS AFTERNOON I WILL:

DATE _____

S M T W T F S

LORD, THANK YOU...
_____
_____
_____

TODAY'S BIBLE READING:

MY DAILY HABITS

- BRUSH TEETH (AM/PM)
- CLEAN ROOM
- READ BIBLE
- PLAY OUTSIDE
- _____
- _____
- _____
- _____

THIS MORNING I WILL:

THIS AFTERNOON I WILL:

DATE _____

S M T W T F S

LORD, THANK YOU...
_____
_____
_____

TODAY'S BIBLE READING:

MY DAILY HABITS

- BRUSH TEETH (AM/PM)
- CLEAN ROOM
- READ BIBLE
- PLAY OUTSIDE
- _____
- _____
- _____
- _____

THIS MORNING I WILL:

THIS AFTERNOON I WILL:

DATE _____

S M T W T F S

LORD, THANK YOU...
_____
_____
_____

TODAY'S BIBLE READING:

MY DAILY HABITS

- BRUSH TEETH (AM/PM)
- CLEAN ROOM
- READ BIBLE
- PLAY OUTSIDE
- _____
- _____
- _____
- _____

THIS MORNING I WILL:

THIS AFTERNOON I WILL:

DATE _____

S M T W T F S

LORD, THANK YOU...

_____
_____
_____

TODAY'S BIBLE READING:

MY DAILY HABITS

- ○ BRUSH TEETH (AM/PM)
- ○ CLEAN ROOM
- ○ READ BIBLE
- ○ PLAY OUTSIDE
- ○ _____
- ○ _____
- ○ _____
- ○ _____

THIS MORNING I WILL:

THIS AFTERNOON I WILL:

DATE _____

S M T W T F S

LORD, THANK YOU...
_____
_____
_____

TODAY'S BIBLE READING:

MY DAILY HABITS

- BRUSH TEETH (AM/PM)
- CLEAN ROOM
- READ BIBLE
- PLAY OUTSIDE
- _____
- _____
- _____
- _____

THIS MORNING I WILL:

THIS AFTERNOON I WILL:

DATE _____

S M T W T F S

LORD, THANK YOU...
_____
_____
_____

TODAY'S BIBLE READING:

MY DAILY HABITS

- BRUSH TEETH (AM/PM)
- CLEAN ROOM
- READ BIBLE
- PLAY OUTSIDE
- _____
- _____
- _____
- _____

THIS MORNING I WILL:

THIS AFTERNOON I WILL:

DATE _____

S M T W T F S

LORD, THANK YOU...
_____
_____
_____

TODAY'S BIBLE READING:

MY DAILY HABITS

- BRUSH TEETH (AM/PM)
- CLEAN ROOM
- READ BIBLE
- PLAY OUTSIDE
- _____
- _____
- _____
- _____

THIS MORNING I WILL:

THIS AFTERNOON I WILL:

DATE _____

S M T W T F S

LORD, THANK YOU...
_____
_____
_____

TODAY'S BIBLE READING:

MY DAILY HABITS

- BRUSH TEETH (AM/PM)
- CLEAN ROOM
- READ BIBLE
- PLAY OUTSIDE
- _____
- _____
- _____
- _____

THIS MORNING I WILL:

THIS AFTERNOON I WILL:

DATE _____

S M T W T F S

LORD, THANK YOU...
_____
_____
_____

Today's Bible Reading:

My Daily Habits

- BRUSH TEETH (AM/PM)
- CLEAN ROOM
- READ BIBLE
- PLAY OUTSIDE
- _____
- _____
- _____
- _____

This Morning I Will:

This Afternoon I Will:

DATE _____

S M T W T F S

LORD, THANK YOU...
_____
_____
_____

TODAY'S BIBLE READING:

MY DAILY HABITS

- BRUSH TEETH (AM/PM)
- CLEAN ROOM
- READ BIBLE
- PLAY OUTSIDE
- _____
- _____
- _____
- _____

THIS MORNING I WILL:

THIS AFTERNOON I WILL:

DATE _____

S M T W T F S

LORD, THANK YOU...
_____
_____
_____

TODAY'S BIBLE READING:

MY DAILY HABITS

- ○ BRUSH TEETH (AM/PM)
- ○ CLEAN ROOM
- ○ READ BIBLE
- ○ PLAY OUTSIDE
- ○ _____
- ○ _____
- ○ _____
- ○ _____

THIS MORNING I WILL:

THIS AFTERNOON I WILL:

DATE _____

S M T W T F S

LORD, THANK YOU...
_____
_____
_____

TODAY'S BIBLE READING:

MY DAILY HABITS

- ○ BRUSH TEETH (AM/PM)
- ○ CLEAN ROOM
- ○ READ BIBLE
- ○ PLAY OUTSIDE
- ○ _____
- ○ _____
- ○ _____
- ○ _____

THIS MORNING I WILL:

THIS AFTERNOON I WILL:

DATE _____

S M T W T F S

LORD, THANK YOU...
_____
_____
_____

TODAY'S BIBLE READING:

MY DAILY HABITS

- ○ BRUSH TEETH (AM/PM)
- ○ CLEAN ROOM
- ○ READ BIBLE
- ○ PLAY OUTSIDE
- ○ _____
- ○ _____
- ○ _____
- ○ _____

THIS MORNING I WILL:

THIS AFTERNOON I WILL:

DATE _____

S M T W T F S

LORD, THANK YOU...
_____
_____
_____

TODAY'S BIBLE READING:

MY DAILY HABITS

- ○ BRUSH TEETH (AM/PM)
- ○ CLEAN ROOM
- ○ READ BIBLE
- ○ PLAY OUTSIDE
- ○ _____
- ○ _____
- ○ _____
- ○ _____

THIS MORNING I WILL:

THIS AFTERNOON I WILL:

DATE _____

S M T W T F S

LORD, THANK YOU...
_____
_____
_____

Today's Bible Reading:

MY DAILY HABITS

- BRUSH TEETH (AM/PM)
- CLEAN ROOM
- READ BIBLE
- PLAY OUTSIDE
- _____
- _____
- _____
- _____

THIS MORNING I WILL:

THIS AFTERNOON I WILL:

DATE _____

S M T W T F S

LORD, THANK YOU...

_____
_____
_____

TODAY'S BIBLE READING:

MY DAILY HABITS

- ○ BRUSH TEETH (AM/PM)
- ○ CLEAN ROOM
- ○ READ BIBLE
- ○ PLAY OUTSIDE
- ○ _____
- ○ _____
- ○ _____
- ○ _____

THIS MORNING I WILL:

THIS AFTERNOON I WILL:

DATE _____

S M T W T F S

LORD, THANK YOU...
_____
_____
_____

TODAY'S BIBLE READING:

MY DAILY HABITS

- ○ BRUSH TEETH (AM/PM)
- ○ CLEAN ROOM
- ○ READ BIBLE
- ○ PLAY OUTSIDE
- ○ _____
- ○ _____
- ○ _____
- ○ _____

THIS MORNING I WILL:

THIS AFTERNOON I WILL:

DATE _____

S M T W T F S

LORD, THANK YOU...
_____
_____
_____

TODAY'S BIBLE READING:

MY DAILY HABITS

- ○ BRUSH TEETH (AM/PM)
- ○ CLEAN ROOM
- ○ READ BIBLE
- ○ PLAY OUTSIDE
- ○ _____
- ○ _____
- ○ _____
- ○ _____

THIS MORNING I WILL:

THIS AFTERNOON I WILL:

DATE _____

S M T W T F S

LORD, THANK YOU...
_____
_____
_____

TODAY'S BIBLE READING:

MY DAILY HABITS

- BRUSH TEETH (AM/PM)
- CLEAN ROOM
- READ BIBLE
- PLAY OUTSIDE
- _____
- _____
- _____
- _____

THIS MORNING I WILL:

THIS AFTERNOON I WILL:

DATE _____

S M T W T F S

LORD, THANK YOU...
_____
_____
_____

TODAY'S BIBLE READING:

MY DAILY HABITS

- BRUSH TEETH (AM/PM)
- CLEAN ROOM
- READ BIBLE
- PLAY OUTSIDE
- _____
- _____
- _____
- _____

THIS MORNING I WILL:

THIS AFTERNOON I WILL:

DATE _____

S M T W T F S

LORD, THANK YOU...
_____
_____
_____

TODAY'S BIBLE READING:

MY DAILY HABITS

- ○ BRUSH TEETH (AM/PM)
- ○ CLEAN ROOM
- ○ READ BIBLE
- ○ PLAY OUTSIDE
- ○ _____
- ○ _____
- ○ _____
- ○ _____

THIS MORNING I WILL:

THIS AFTERNOON I WILL:

DATE _____

S M T W T F S

LORD, THANK YOU...
_____
_____
_____

Today's Bible Reading:

MY DAILY HABITS

- ○ BRUSH TEETH (AM/PM)
- ○ CLEAN ROOM
- ○ READ BIBLE
- ○ PLAY OUTSIDE
- ○ _____
- ○ _____
- ○ _____
- ○ _____

THIS MORNING I WILL:

THIS AFTERNOON I WILL:

DATE _____

S M T W T F S

LORD, THANK YOU...
_____
_____
_____

TODAY'S BIBLE READING:

MY DAILY HABITS

- BRUSH TEETH (AM/PM)
- CLEAN ROOM
- READ BIBLE
- PLAY OUTSIDE
- _____
- _____
- _____
- _____

THIS MORNING I WILL:

THIS AFTERNOON I WILL:

DATE _____

S M T W T F S

LORD, THANK YOU...
_____
_____
_____

TODAY'S BIBLE READING:

MY DAILY HABITS

- ○ BRUSH TEETH (AM/PM)
- ○ CLEAN ROOM
- ○ READ BIBLE
- ○ PLAY OUTSIDE
- ○ _____
- ○ _____
- ○ _____
- ○ _____

THIS MORNING I WILL:

THIS AFTERNOON I WILL:

DATE _____

S M T W T F S

LORD, THANK YOU...
_____
_____
_____

TODAY'S BIBLE READING:

MY DAILY HABITS

- ○ BRUSH TEETH (AM/PM)
- ○ CLEAN ROOM
- ○ READ BIBLE
- ○ PLAY OUTSIDE
- ○ _____
- ○ _____
- ○ _____
- ○ _____

THIS MORNING I WILL:

THIS AFTERNOON I WILL:

DATE _____

S M T W T F S

LORD, THANK YOU...
_____
_____
_____

Today's Bible Reading:

My Daily Habits

- ○ BRUSH TEETH (AM/PM)
- ○ CLEAN ROOM
- ○ READ BIBLE
- ○ PLAY OUTSIDE
- ○ _____
- ○ _____
- ○ _____
- ○ _____

This Morning I Will:

This Afternoon I Will:

DATE _____

S M T W T F S

LORD, THANK YOU...
_____
_____
_____

Today's Bible Reading:

MY DAILY HABITS

- BRUSH TEETH (AM/PM)
- CLEAN ROOM
- READ BIBLE
- PLAY OUTSIDE
- _____
- _____
- _____
- _____

THIS MORNING I WILL:

THIS AFTERNOON I WILL:

DATE _____

S M T W T F S

LORD, THANK YOU...
_____
_____
_____

TODAY'S BIBLE READING:

MY DAILY HABITS

- ○ BRUSH TEETH (AM/PM)
- ○ CLEAN ROOM
- ○ READ BIBLE
- ○ PLAY OUTSIDE
- ○ _____
- ○ _____
- ○ _____
- ○ _____

THIS MORNING I WILL:

THIS AFTERNOON I WILL:

DATE _____

S M T W T F S

LORD, THANK YOU...
_____
_____
_____

Today's Bible Reading:

My Daily Habits

- BRUSH TEETH (AM/PM)
- CLEAN ROOM
- READ BIBLE
- PLAY OUTSIDE
- _____
- _____
- _____
- _____

This Morning I Will:

This Afternoon I Will:

DATE _____

S M T W T F S

LORD, THANK YOU...
_____
_____
_____

TODAY'S BIBLE READING:

MY DAILY HABITS

- ○ BRUSH TEETH (AM/PM)
- ○ CLEAN ROOM
- ○ READ BIBLE
- ○ PLAY OUTSIDE
- ○ _____
- ○ _____
- ○ _____
- ○ _____

THIS MORNING I WILL:

THIS AFTERNOON I WILL:

DATE _____

S M T W T F S

LORD, THANK YOU...
_____
_____
_____

TODAY'S BIBLE READING:

MY DAILY HABITS

- BRUSH TEETH (AM/PM)
- CLEAN ROOM
- READ BIBLE
- PLAY OUTSIDE
- _____
- _____
- _____
- _____

THIS MORNING I WILL:

THIS AFTERNOON I WILL:

DATE _____

S M T W T F S

LORD, THANK YOU...
_____
_____
_____

Today's Bible Reading:

My Daily Habits

- BRUSH TEETH (AM/PM)
- CLEAN ROOM
- READ BIBLE
- PLAY OUTSIDE
- _____
- _____
- _____
- _____

This Morning I Will:

This Afternoon I Will:

DATE _____

S M T W T F S

LORD, THANK YOU...
_____
_____
_____

Today's Bible Reading:

MY DAILY HABITS

- BRUSH TEETH (AM/PM)
- CLEAN ROOM
- READ BIBLE
- PLAY OUTSIDE
- _____
- _____
- _____
- _____

THIS MORNING I WILL:

THIS AFTERNOON I WILL:

DATE _____

S M T W T F S

LORD, THANK YOU...
_____
_____
_____

Today's Bible Reading:

My Daily Habits

- ⚪ BRUSH TEETH (AM/PM)
- ⚪ CLEAN ROOM
- ⚪ READ BIBLE
- ⚪ PLAY OUTSIDE
- ⚪ _____
- ⚪ _____
- ⚪ _____
- ⚪ _____

This Morning I Will:

This Afternoon I Will:

DATE _____

S M T W T F S

LORD, THANK YOU...
_____
_____
_____

TODAY'S BIBLE READING:

MY DAILY HABITS

- BRUSH TEETH (AM/PM)
- CLEAN ROOM
- READ BIBLE
- PLAY OUTSIDE
- _____
- _____
- _____
- _____

THIS MORNING I WILL:

THIS AFTERNOON I WILL:

DATE _____

S M T W T F S

LORD, THANK YOU...
_____
_____
_____

TODAY'S BIBLE READING:

MY DAILY HABITS

- ○ BRUSH TEETH (AM/PM)
- ○ CLEAN ROOM
- ○ READ BIBLE
- ○ PLAY OUTSIDE
- ○ _____
- ○ _____
- ○ _____
- ○ _____

THIS MORNING I WILL:

THIS AFTERNOON I WILL:

DATE _____

S M T W T F S

LORD, THANK YOU...
_____
_____
_____

TODAY'S BIBLE READING:

MY DAILY HABITS

- BRUSH TEETH (AM/PM)
- CLEAN ROOM
- READ BIBLE
- PLAY OUTSIDE
- _____
- _____
- _____
- _____

THIS MORNING I WILL:

THIS AFTERNOON I WILL:

Date _____

S M T W T F S

LORD, THANK YOU...
_____
_____
_____

Today's Bible Reading:

My Daily Habits

- BRUSH TEETH (AM/PM)
- CLEAN ROOM
- READ BIBLE
- PLAY OUTSIDE
- _____
- _____
- _____
- _____

This Morning I Will:

This Afternoon I Will:

DATE _____

S M T W T F S

LORD, THANK YOU...

_____
_____
_____

Today's Bible Reading:

MY DAILY HABITS

- BRUSH TEETH (AM/PM)
- CLEAN ROOM
- READ BIBLE
- PLAY OUTSIDE
- _____
- _____
- _____
- _____

THIS MORNING I WILL:

THIS AFTERNOON I WILL:

DATE _____

S M T W T F S

LORD, THANK YOU...
_____
_____
_____

TODAY'S BIBLE READING:

MY DAILY HABITS

- ○ BRUSH TEETH (AM/PM)
- ○ CLEAN ROOM
- ○ READ BIBLE
- ○ PLAY OUTSIDE
- ○ _____
- ○ _____
- ○ _____
- ○ _____

THIS MORNING I WILL:

THIS AFTERNOON I WILL:

DATE _____

S M T W T F S

LORD, THANK YOU...
_____
_____
_____

TODAY'S BIBLE READING:

MY DAILY HABITS

- BRUSH TEETH (AM/PM)
- CLEAN ROOM
- READ BIBLE
- PLAY OUTSIDE
- _____
- _____
- _____
- _____

THIS MORNING I WILL:

THIS AFTERNOON I WILL:

DATE _____

S M T W T F S

LORD, THANK YOU...
_____
_____
_____

TODAY'S BIBLE READING:

MY DAILY HABITS

- ○ BRUSH TEETH (AM/PM)
- ○ CLEAN ROOM
- ○ READ BIBLE
- ○ PLAY OUTSIDE
- ○ _____
- ○ _____
- ○ _____
- ○ _____

THIS MORNING I WILL:

THIS AFTERNOON I WILL:

DATE _____

S M T W T F S

LORD, THANK YOU...
_____
_____
_____

TODAY'S BIBLE READING:

MY DAILY HABITS

- ○ BRUSH TEETH (AM/PM)
- ○ CLEAN ROOM
- ○ READ BIBLE
- ○ PLAY OUTSIDE
- ○ _____
- ○ _____
- ○ _____
- ○ _____

THIS MORNING I WILL:

THIS AFTERNOON I WILL:

DATE _____

S M T W T F S

LORD, THANK YOU...
_____
_____
_____

TODAY'S BIBLE READING:

MY DAILY HABITS

- ○ BRUSH TEETH (AM/PM)
- ○ CLEAN ROOM
- ○ READ BIBLE
- ○ PLAY OUTSIDE
- ○ _____
- ○ _____
- ○ _____
- ○ _____

THIS MORNING I WILL:

THIS AFTERNOON I WILL:

DATE _____

S M T W T F S

LORD, THANK YOU...
_____
_____
_____

Today's Bible Reading:

My Daily Habits

- BRUSH TEETH (AM/PM)
- CLEAN ROOM
- READ BIBLE
- PLAY OUTSIDE
- _____
- _____
- _____
- _____

This Morning I Will:

This Afternoon I Will:

DATE _____

S M T W T F S

LORD, THANK YOU...
_____
_____
_____

TODAY'S BIBLE READING:

MY DAILY HABITS

- ○ BRUSH TEETH (AM/PM)
- ○ CLEAN ROOM
- ○ READ BIBLE
- ○ PLAY OUTSIDE
- ○ _____
- ○ _____
- ○ _____
- ○ _____

THIS MORNING I WILL:

THIS AFTERNOON I WILL:

DATE _____

S M T W T F S

LORD, THANK YOU...
_____
_____
_____

Today's Bible Reading:

My Daily Habits

- ○ BRUSH TEETH (AM/PM)
- ○ CLEAN ROOM
- ○ READ BIBLE
- ○ PLAY OUTSIDE
- ○ _____
- ○ _____
- ○ _____
- ○ _____

This Morning I Will:

This Afternoon I Will:

DATE _____

S M T W T F S

LORD, THANK YOU...
_____
_____
_____

TODAY'S BIBLE READING:

MY DAILY HABITS

- BRUSH TEETH (AM/PM)
- CLEAN ROOM
- READ BIBLE
- PLAY OUTSIDE
- _____
- _____
- _____
- _____

THIS MORNING I WILL:

THIS AFTERNOON I WILL:

Date _____

S M T W T F S

Lord, thank you...
_____
_____
_____

Today's Bible Reading:

My Daily Habits

- BRUSH TEETH (AM/PM)
- CLEAN ROOM
- READ BIBLE
- PLAY OUTSIDE
- _____
- _____
- _____
- _____

This Morning I Will:

This Afternoon I Will:

DATE _____

S M T W T F S

LORD, THANK YOU...
_____
_____
_____

Today's Bible Reading:

My Daily Habits

- BRUSH TEETH (AM/PM)
- CLEAN ROOM
- READ BIBLE
- PLAY OUTSIDE
- _____
- _____
- _____
- _____

This Morning I Will:

This Afternoon I Will:

DATE _____

S M T W T F S

LORD, THANK YOU...
_____
_____
_____

Today's Bible Reading:

My Daily Habits

- ○ BRUSH TEETH (AM/PM)
- ○ CLEAN ROOM
- ○ READ BIBLE
- ○ PLAY OUTSIDE
- ○ _____
- ○ _____
- ○ _____
- ○ _____

This Morning I Will:

This Afternoon I Will:

Date _____

S M T W T F S

LORD, THANK YOU...
_____
_____
_____

Today's Bible Reading:

My Daily Habits

- BRUSH TEETH (AM/PM)
- CLEAN ROOM
- READ BIBLE
- PLAY OUTSIDE
- _____
- _____
- _____
- _____

This Morning I Will:

This Afternoon I Will:

DATE _____

S M T W T F S

LORD, THANK YOU...
_____
_____
_____

TODAY'S BIBLE READING:

MY DAILY HABITS

- ○ BRUSH TEETH (AM/PM)
- ○ CLEAN ROOM
- ○ READ BIBLE
- ○ PLAY OUTSIDE
- ○ _____
- ○ _____
- ○ _____
- ○ _____

THIS MORNING I WILL:

THIS AFTERNOON I WILL:

DATE _____

S M T W T F S

LORD, THANK YOU...

_____
_____
_____

TODAY'S BIBLE READING:

MY DAILY HABITS

- BRUSH TEETH (AM/PM)
- CLEAN ROOM
- READ BIBLE
- PLAY OUTSIDE
- _____
- _____
- _____
- _____

THIS MORNING I WILL:

THIS AFTERNOON I WILL:

DATE ____

S M T W T F S

LORD, THANK YOU...
_____
_____
_____

TODAY'S BIBLE READING:

MY DAILY HABITS

- BRUSH TEETH (AM/PM)
- CLEAN ROOM
- READ BIBLE
- PLAY OUTSIDE
- _____
- _____
- _____
- _____

THIS MORNING I WILL:

THIS AFTERNOON I WILL:

DATE _____

S M T W T F S

LORD, THANK YOU...
_____
_____
_____

TODAY'S BIBLE READING:

MY DAILY HABITS

- BRUSH TEETH (AM/PM)
- CLEAN ROOM
- READ BIBLE
- PLAY OUTSIDE
- _____
- _____
- _____
- _____

THIS MORNING I WILL:

THIS AFTERNOON I WILL:

JUNE

MONDAY	TUESDAY	WEDNESDAY	THURSDAY	FRIDAY	SATURDAY	SUNDAY

NOTES

JULY

MONDAY	TUESDAY	WEDNESDAY	THURSDAY	FRIDAY	SATURDAY	SUNDAY

NOTES

AUGUST

MONDAY	TUESDAY	WEDNESDAY	THURSDAY	FRIDAY	SATURDAY	SUNDAY

NOTES

WHAT TO DO IF YOU ARE BORED:

PHYSICAL THINGS:

JUMP ON A TRAMPOLINE
DANCE TO DISNEY MUSIC
PLAY TAG WITH YOUR SIBLINGS
GO ON A WALK
DO PUSH-UPS AND SIT-UPS
DO A WORKOUT ON YOUTUBE
PLAY CATCH WITH YOUR DOG
FRISBEE
FRISBEE GOLF
4-SQUARE
HULA HOOP
MAKE A NINJA COURSE
RUN THROUGH THE SPRINKLER
HOP SCOTCH
TRAIN FOR A RACE
PLAY AT THE PARK
CLIMB A TREE
MOW THE GRASS
CLEAN UP YOUR YARD
RIDE YOUR BIKE
HIKE
ROLLER BLADE
JUMP ROPE
CAPTURE THE FLAG
COLLECT TREASURES ON A WALK
BASKETBALL
FLAG FOOTBALL
SOCCER
VOLLEYBALL
LEARN A NEW SPORT
GO SWIMMING
GO BOWLING
THREE-LEGGED RACE
RACE
WASH THE CAR
MAKE-UP A SCAVENGER HUNT
PRACTICE DOING PULL-UPS
SET A TIMER & DO A CHALLENGE
GYMNASTICS
STRETCHING OR YOGA
BUILD A FORT

CREATIVE THINGS:

DRAW OR COLOR
MAKE A PAPER AIRPLANE
WRITE A BOOK
PLAY WITH LEGOS
MAKE-UP A SONG
PLAY AN INSTRUMENT
MAKE A YOUTUBE VIDEO
BAKE COOKIES
PAINT A PICTURE
COLOR WITH SIDEWALK CHALK
WRITE A LETTER TO A GRANDPARENT
MAKE A CRAFT OUT OF CARDBOARD
MAKE JEWELRY WITH BEADS
BUILD A FORT OUT OF BLANKETS
PLANT SOME FLOWERS
MAKE A FAIRY GARDEN
BUILD A BIRDHOUSE
HAVE A TEA PARTY
MAKE A COLLAGE FROM MAGAZINES
PUT TOGETHER A PUZZLE
LEARN HOW TO WRITE FANCY LETTERS
MAKE A COMIC
PUT ON A PLAY
DESIGN A GARDEN
ORIGAMI
LEARN HOW TO MAKE A NEW FOOD
LEARN A NEW LANGUAGE
WRITE A POEM
MAKE AND PLAY WITH PLAYDOUGH
PLAY WITH TOYS YOU FORGOT ABOUT
PAINT ROCKS
SEW A PILLOW
PLAY A BOARD GAME
READ
LEARN NEW HAIRSTYLES
ORGANIZE YOUR CLOSET
REARRANGE YOUR ROOM
MAKE A ROBOT FROM TRASH
DO A SCIENCE EXPERIMENT
FIND, AND WRITE TO, A PEN PAL
KEEP A JOURNAL ABOUT YOUR DAY
SIT OUTSIDE AND SKETCH WHAT YOU SEE

MY OWN IDEAS:

My prayer is that this Bible study/daily planner has helped you grow in your relationship with the Lord, and encouraged you to live each day with purpose.

To continue the habit of spending time in the Word each day, check out:

DIGGING into GOD

www.diggingintoGod.com

DIG

Copyright © 2021 by Heather Coppinger

Made in the USA
Columbia, SC
18 June 2025